TO: My Friend Mary Ann

FROM: Brenda

WHY Because you've been my friend and you helped me more than you know to keep on dancing.

I HOPE YOU DANCE

MARK D. SANDERS AND TIA SILLERS

INTRODUCTION BY LEE ANN WOMACK

RUTLEDGE HILL PRESS® • NASHVILLE, TENNESSEE

A THOMAS NELSON COMPANY

WE, MARK AND TIA, WOULD LIKE
TO DEDICATE THIS BOOK TO OUR FAMILIES.

I HOPE YOU DANCE

I hope you never lose your sense of wonder
You get your fill to eat but always keep that hunger
May you never take one single breath for granted
God forbid love ever leave you empty-handed
I hope you still feel small when you stand beside the ocean
Whenever one door closes I hope one more opens
Promise me that you'll give faith a fighting chance
And when you get the choice to sit it out or dance
I hope you dance. . . I hope you dance
I hope you never fear those mountains in the distance
Never settle for the path of least resistance
Livin' might mean takin' chances but they're worth takin'
Lovin' might be a mistake but it's worth makin'
Don't let some hell-bent heart leave you bitter
When you come close to sellin' out reconsider
Give the heavens above more than just a passing glance
And when you get the choice to sit it out or dance
I hope you dance. . . I hope you dance
Time is a wheel in constant motion always rolling us along.
Tell me who wants to look back on their years and wonder
where those years have gone.
I hope you dance. . . I hope you dance
I hope you dance

When I heard the lyric of "I Hope You Dance" the first time, my children came to mind immediately. These are the things I want for them in life: to feel small when they stand beside the ocean, to give faith a fighting chance, to give the heavens above more than just a passing glance. I remember thinking, "If they understand the meaning of this lyric when they're grown, I'll have done my job as their mother."

I had nothing to do with the writing of this song or this book, but, thankfully, I've been asked to be a part of both. Mark and Tia have done a beautiful job—as our writers in Nashville are known to do—of putting into words the very things that the rest of us want and need to say but aren't quite sure how. They are masters of their craft and I consider myself truly blessed to have been the vehicle to bring their song to so many millions of people.

LEE ANN WOMACK

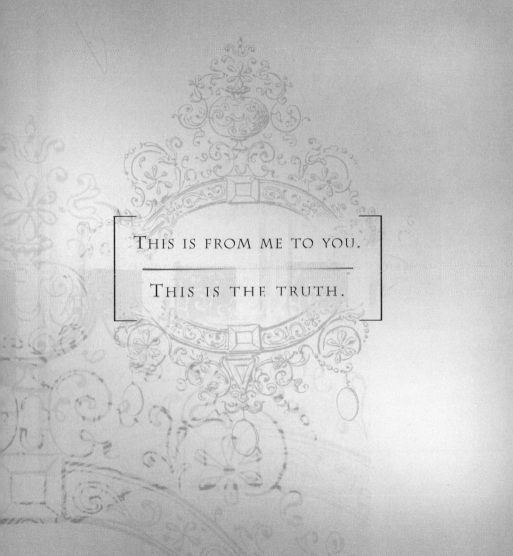

THIS IS FROM ME TO YOU.

THIS IS THE TRUTH.

How many times have
my wishes
and my dreams
and my prayers
for you
hidden beneath my breath?

How many times have I looked at you,
heart in my throat,
hands in my pockets,
a smile on my face,
just wanting to say...

I HOPE
LOSE YOUR
OF

What is hope?
To want? To desire?
To expect that what's envisioned
may indeed happen?
YES to all of the above.
Is hope that gut feeling that it's
worth holding out
and hanging on for just a little longer?
ABSOLUTELY.
Is hope the core of the human condition?
CERTAINLY.
Can you have hope without
faith and humility and wonder?
THAT'S TOUGH.
Just the thought that there's something bigger,
something truer, something totally surprising
out there waiting for us is...
priceless.

What would you be without hope
growing deep in your bones,
thriving in every inch of you?

N O T H I N G.

WHAT DOES IT TAKE TO HOPE?

EVERYTHING

Hope takes never ceasing
to be amazed...

Wearing
your soul on your sleeve...

Holding
your breath, waiting to hear
"I love you, too..."

Believing
that tomorrow could be better than today...
that you'll get a second chance...
that you'll make a difference...
that you matter.

YOU GET YOUR FILL TO EAT
BUT ALWAYS KEEP THAT HUNGER

Hunger is the wanting:
  to see more
  to feel more
  to touch more
  to crave, desire, search out, find, hold more.
And sometimes hunger hurts more.
But go on, go west, young man, young woman.
Plow the land,
plant the seeds,
grow the food for the whole wide world.

MAY YOU
TAKE ONE
BREATH FOR

NEVER
SINGLE
GRANTED

SO BREATHE OUT AND BREATHE IN

(AND SOAK IT ALL UP)

GOD FORBID LOVE EVER LEAVE YOU EMPTY-HANDED

But if it does,

may it leave you patient and stronger,

willing* and wiser, tender and tougher.

* WONDERFUL WORD CONTRIBUTED BY SOPHIE SANDERS, AGE 10, THEN

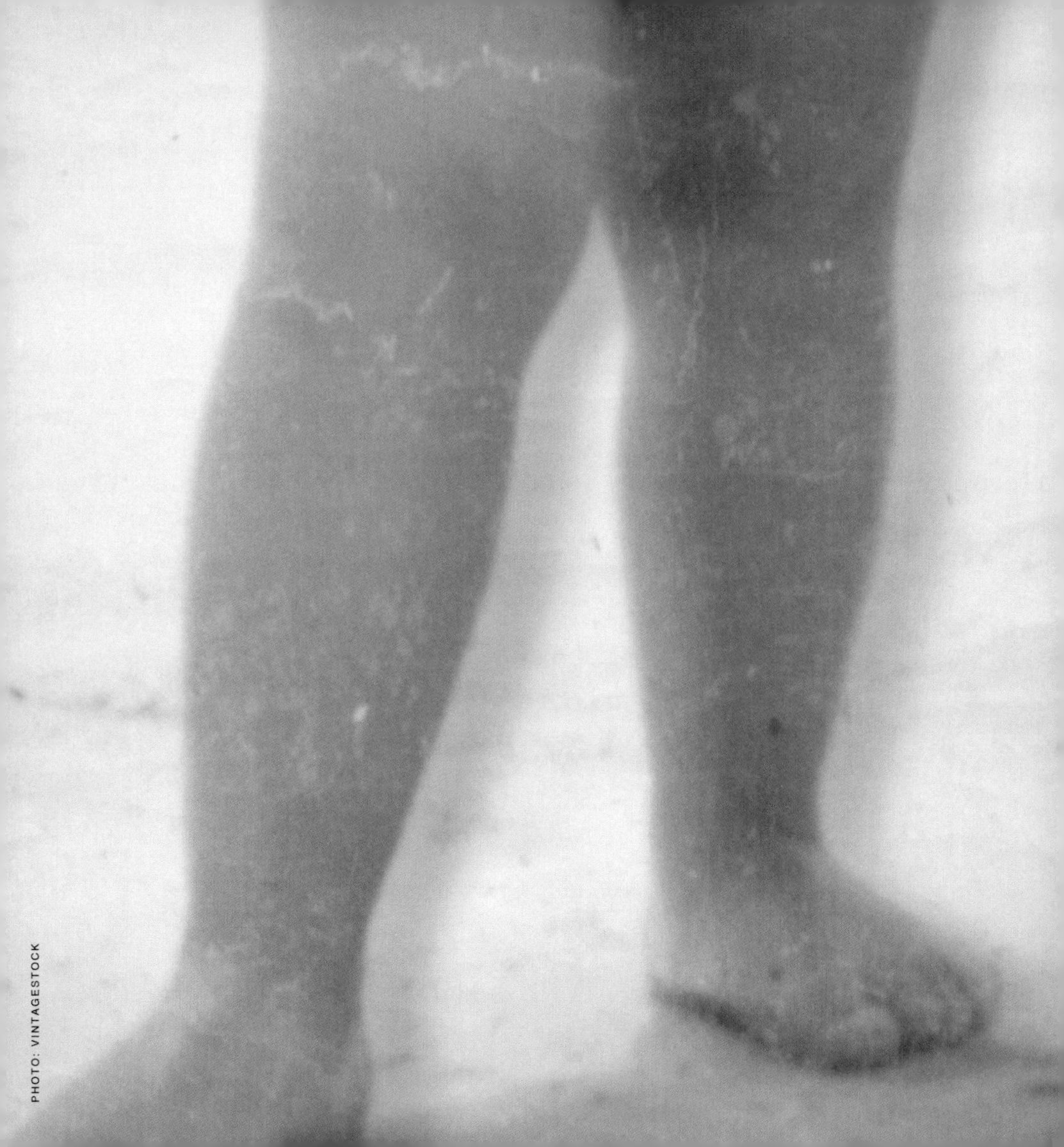

PHOTO: VINTAGESTOCK

I HOPE YOU
STILL FEEL

SMALL

WHEN YOU
STAND BESIDE
THE OCEAN

If you're ever lying on a beach with

80 billion* grains of sand beneath you,

700 thousand* ocean waves before you,

60 million* stars stretched out above you,

and you're still not at all impressed,

I want you to think about this:

The light you see reflecting from the stars is over one million* years old.

WOW.

But then, just before you start to feel like a mere blip

in the gigantic scheme of things, please remember this:

Yes, you are small, but you're also irreplaceable

and invaluable

and miraculous.

Those stars don't have anything on you.

*ALL NUMBERS GROSSLY UNDERESTIMATED.

WHENEVER
ONE
DOOR CLOSES
I HOPE
ONE MORE
OPENS

DOORS

Holes in walls that offer us a way out or a way in.
Just putting your hand on the knob and seeing if it turns can
make you weak in the knees.

What if it's locked?
What if it's unlocked?
What if no one answers?
What if someone does?

What if the hinges creak and the heavy wood swings
open
and you're suddenly standing at the threshold
of a brand new tomorrow?
What if your horizon is nothing but
blue clear skies?
What if it's a raging storm?
What if?
What if?

What if?

PROMISE
YOU'LL GIVE
FIGHTING

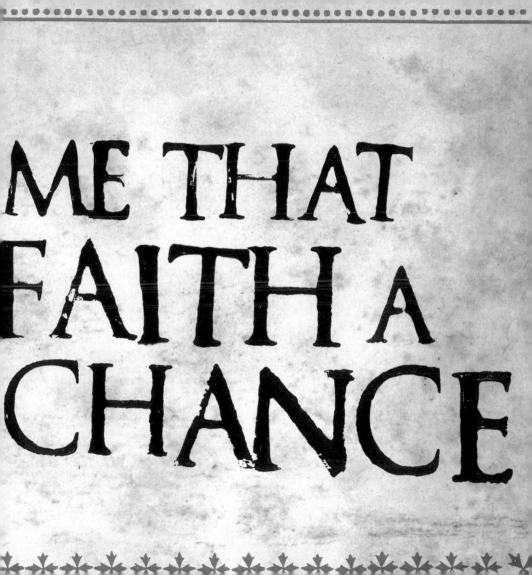

A PROMISE IS ALL ABOUT FAITH.
A PROMISE IS ONLY AS STRONG
as your own faith in your own self,
in your own god.
So when you swear,
in light of your strengths and in spite
of your weaknesses,
to struggle and follow through,
you
are doing a beautiful thing.

AND WHEN CHOICE IT OUT

YOU GET THE
TO SIT
OR DANCE

Let the music move you,
let the moment take your hand,
let it lead you out into
the middle of the dance floor and
embrace you.
Dive off the high board,
ride with the top down,
thrive like a wildflower,
and sing
(who cares what you sound like)
with a voice all your own.

I HOPE YOU NEVER
FEAR THOSE MOUNTAINS
IN THE DISTANCE

It's crossing your fingers when the map doesn't make sense, when the compass oesn't know truly north from truly lost; and it's up to you–you and your gut and your mettle, and your level of resilience, and your wealth of wisdom– to persevere. To get to the other side.

To hope.

NEVER
FOR THE
LEAST

SETTLE

PATH OF

RESISTANCE

(THAT'S TOO EASY. WHAT FOLLOWS IS TOO INTERESTING.)

LIVING MIGHT
MEAN TAKING
CHANCES,
BUT THEY'RE
WORTH TAKING

Ask Eve.

Evolve.

Take a chance, take a ticket,

take a fast train to the coast.

No guts, no glory.

Chance (n.): a coin with two sides that one tosses into the air as many times as one wants. The odds remain the same.

It's risky breathing, let alone needing,

trusting, reaching out. Life is the leap of faith,

the bold declaration of

<u>Hope.</u>

Attention

This is REALLY BIG Stuff! This is the crux of the whole adventure!

LOVING MIGHT BE A MISTAKE, BUT IT'S WORTH MAKING

LOVE, LOVE, LOVE.

YOU HAVE TO LOVE,

AND IF YOU DON'T GET LOVE RIGHT,

YOU HAVE TO MOVE ON

AND FORGIVE.

AND THEN YOU HAVE TO REMEMBER

THAT YOU'VE FORGIVEN,

OR ELSE YOU CAN'T MOVE ON.

AND IF YOU DON'T MOVE ON,

YOU'LL SURELY END UP. . .

BITTER.*

* SEE NEXT PAGE

DON'T
LET SOME
HELL-BENT
HEART
LEAVE
YOU BITTER

(AND DON'T SAY I DIDN'T WARN YOU)

There are too many people too angry

at a world that isn't

in the least bit angry at them.

WHEN YOU COME
CLOSE TO SELLING OUT,
RECONSIDER

YOU

(A HAIKU)

One worth so much

to me, to us, to life as such.

A bowl of cherries.

GIVE THE HEAVENS ABOVE MORE THAN JUST A PASSING GLANCE

Heaven (n.): (1) a place somehow high above the clouds, yet deep inside your soul; (2) a place of complete peace, of total and utter happiness; (3) a place that is greater than the sum of everything you will ever be or could ever imagine to be; (4) a place we all want to get to, but just not yet...

NO, NOT YET.

AND WHEN YOU GET THE CHOICE TO SIT IT OUT OR DANCE ...

(AS YOU NOW WELL KNOW)

I HOPE YOU DANCE BECAUSE

Time.

Time is a wheel.

Time is a wheel in constant motion

always

rolling us along.

Tell me who wants to look back on their years and wonder. . .

WHERE THEIR YEARS HAVE GONE

Ah, youth...new skin, wide smiles,
clear eyes...the future so bright.
If only we could bottle it, sip it now and
again, and stay forever twenty-one,
forever ten, forever five.

I liked being five.

But I'd also like to think that time and age are like cousins—
they're relative.
Who said you have to go by actual miles?
If you didn't know how old you were, how old would you be?
(me, I'm sticking with five.)

I'll even argue that you can bottle youth.
What you store it in is all up to you.
(I suggest your heart.)
If you can figure out a way to keep
the energy and gumption and fire alive,
you'll always stay young.
And where there's youth, there's hope. . .
where there's hope, there's wonder. . .
where there's wonder, there's faith. . .
where there's faith, there's chance. . .
where there's chance, there's love. . .
where there's love, there's music. . .
and dancing.

SO IN MY HEART OF HEARTS

I HOPE YOU DANCE

I REALLY
HOPE YOU
DANCE

Amen.

PROMISE ME ONE MORE THING:

If tomorrow you wake up feeling

unoriginal

or

frail-hearted

or

faithless

or

tired of this world

please

pick up this book and start back at page

ONE.

(OR JUST CALL ME.)

NO, IT'S NOT THE END.

IT'S THE BEGINNING.